Senior Art Editor Anna Formanek
Project Editor Lara Hutcheson
Managing Editor Tori Kosara
Managing Art Editor Jo Connor
Designer Emma Wicks
Production Editor Siu Yin Chan
Senior Production Controller Lloyd Robertson
Publisher Paula Regan
Art Director Charlotte Coulais
Managing Director Mark Searle

Written by Lara Hutcheson
Designed for DK by Thelma-Jane Robb
Reading Consultant Barbara Marinak

DK would like to thank Hank Woon, Alyssa Tuffey, and the rest of the team at The Pokémon Company International. Thanks also to Lori Hand for proofreading.

First American Edition, 2025
Published in the United States by DK Publishing,
a division of Penguin Random House LLC
1745 Broadway, 20th Floor, New York, NY 10019
25 26 27 28 29 10 9 8 7 6 5 4 3 2 1
001–344860–Jul/2025

© 2025 Pokémon. © 1997–2023 Nintendo, Creatures, GAME FREAK,
TV Tokyo, ShoPro, JR Kikaku. TM, ® Nintendo.

All rights reserved.
Without limiting the rights under the copyright reserved above, no part of this publication may be reproduced, stored in or introduced into a retrieval system, or transmitted, in any form, or by any means (electronic, mechanical, photocopying, recording, or otherwise), without the prior written permission of the copyright owner.
Published in Great Britain by Dorling Kindersley Limited

A catalog record for this book
is available from the Library of Congress.
ISBN 978-0-5939-6582-5 (Paperback)
ISBN 978-0-5939-6583-2 (Hardcover)

DK books are available at special discounts when purchased
in bulk for sales promotions, premiums, fund-raising, or educational use.
For details, contact: DK Publishing Special Markets,
1745 Broadway, 20th Floor, New York, NY 10019
SpecialSales@dk.com

Printed and bound in China

www.dk.com
www.pokemon.com

This book was made with Forest Stewardship Council™ certified paper—one small step in DK's commitment to a sustainable future. Learn more at www.dk.com/uk/information/sustainability

Level 2

Pokémon

Ready, Set, Catch!

DK

Contents

6	Catching Pokémon
8	Friede's team
10	Finding Pokémon
12	Wild Pokémon
14	Poké Balls
16	Be prepared
18	Rotom Phone
20	Battle time
22	Know your types
24	Winning moves
26	Perfect partners
28	Never give up
30	Glossary
31	Index
32	Quiz

Catching Pokémon

Pokémon Trainers like to catch lots of Pokémon. They hope to make a strong team.

The strongest teams will often include Pokémon that have a range of different skills in battle.

Pokémon Trainer, Spinel

Beheeyem

Beheeyem can control opponents' memories.

Umbreon

Umbreon has a powerful battle move called "Snarl."

Friede's team

Friede's team includes Captain Pikachu and Charizard. They are always happy to help each other out.

Working together
Captain Pikachu helps Friede on the airship, *The Brave Olivine*.

Catch a ride

Friede can travel on Charizard's back.

Brave and fierce

Together the team is strong in battle.

Finding Pokémon

Pokémon can be found in all sorts of places.

Some Pokémon like to come out at night, while others prefer the day.

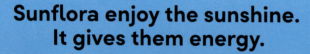
Sunflora enjoy the sunshine. It gives them energy.

Eyes can see in the dark

Noctowl like to come out at night.

Places to look for Pokémon
- Forests and fields
- Lakes and seas
- Caves
- Trees

Wild Pokémon

Would you like to catch a wild Pokémon?

They are found all over the Pokémon world, if you know where to look for them!

Finding Combee

Look for Combee near flowers. They like to gather nectar.

Forest friends

You can find Jumpluff, Skiddo, and Venomoth in Arboliva's Forest.

Poké Balls

A Poké Ball is used to catch Pokémon.

Roy

Poké Ball

Some Poké Balls are better at catching certain Pokémon than others.

Ultra Ball

Great Ball

Master Ball

Ancient Poké Ball

A good Trainer knows which Poké Ball to use.

Be prepared

Sometimes a Poké Ball isn't the only thing you need to be able to catch Pokémon.

Ludlow and his fishing rod.

A fishing rod can be used to catch Pokémon in the water.

You can also use tasty berries and snacks to tempt Pokémon out from hiding.

Finding berries makes Chansey happy.

Rotom Phone

The Rotom Phone is a useful device. It includes a Pokédex.

A Pokédex is packed with facts about Pokémon.

Rotom Phone can:

- Identify a Pokémon
- Give their height, weight, and type
- Provide facts about their habitat and needs
- Tell you about their battle style

Rotom Phone

Liko and Roy were given a Rotom Phone at the start of their Pokémon journey.

On screen

This Rotom Phone is showing a Pokémon called Doliv.

Battle time

Pokémon are easier to catch if they are weakened first in battle.

They only want to be caught by a strong Trainer!

Liko wants to be brave in battle.

Sprigatito vs. Galarian Moltres

Liko's Sprigatito used a battle move called Leafage to calm Galarian Moltres.

Know your types

In battle, it is good to know what types of Pokémon are strong or weak against others.

Sharp claws

Golduck

Webbed feet

A Water type, like Golduck, can be strong against a Fire type, like Slugma.

23

Winning moves

Rock types, like Sudowoodo, are often strong against Fire types, like Fuecoco.

Sudowoodo's Rock Throw

This Rock-type move caught Roy and Fuecoco by surprise!

Worn out

Fuecoco did its best, but it was beaten in battle.

Roy's regret

Roy wished he had known more about his opponent.

Perfect partners

Not all Pokémon are hard to catch. Dot chose her friend Quaxly to be her first Pokémon.

They did not have to battle because Quaxly was very happy to be chosen.

Dot and Quaxly

Dot's Poké Ball

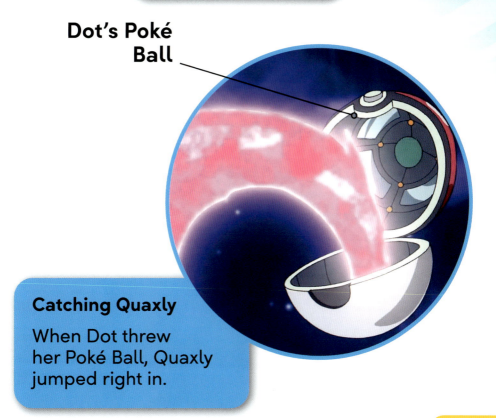

Catching Quaxly

When Dot threw her Poké Ball, Quaxly jumped right in.

Never give up

There are so many amazing Pokémon to discover. Keep on searching.

Build a top Pokémon team and get ready for your next adventure!

Friends together

Glossary

Device
An invention or machine used for a special purpose.

Habitat
The natural environment of an animal or plant.

Nectar
Sweet liquid found in flowers.

Opponent
Someone who is competing against another.

Poké Ball
A ball used by Trainers to catch and carry Pokémon.

Pokémon Trainer
Someone who raises Pokémon and battles with them in competition.

Tempt
To make someone want to do something.

Index

A
Ancient Poké Ball 15
Arboliva's Forest 13

B
Beheeyem 7
The Brave Olivine 8

C
Captain Pikachu 8
Chansey 17
Charizard 8–9
Combee 13

D
Doliv 19
Dot 26–27

F
Fire type 23, 24–25
Friede 8–9
Fuecoco 24–25

G
Galarian Moltres 21
Golduck 22–23
Great Ball 15

J
Jumpluff 12–13

L
Leafage 21
Liko 19, 20–21
Ludlow 16

M
Master Ball 15

N
Noctowl 11

P
Poké Balls 14–15, 27
Pokémon Trainers 6

Q
Quaxly 26–27

R
Rock type 24–25
Rotom Phone 18–19
Roy 14, 19, 25

S
Skiddo 12–13
Slugma 23
Snarl 7
Spinel 6
Sprigatito 21
Sudowoodo 24
Sunflora 10

U
Ultra Ball 15
Umbreon 7

V
Venomoth 13

W
Water type 22–23
Wild Pokémon 12–13

Quiz

It's time to find out how much you have learned! Read the questions and then check the answers with an adult.

1. What gives Sunflora energy?

2. Does Umbreon have a battle move called "Snarl"?

3. Can a Rotom Phone be used to identify Pokémon?

4. Is Slugma a Water-type Pokémon?

5. Which Pokémon was Dot's first ever catch?

1. Sunshine 2. Yes 3. Yes 4. No, it is a Fire type 5. Quaxly